UNDERSTANDING PSYCHOLOGY

Understanding
Motivation

Understanding
Motivation

Kris Hirschmann

San Diego, CA

© 2018 ReferencePoint Press, Inc.
Printed in the United States

For more information, contact:
ReferencePoint Press, Inc.
PO Box 27779
San Diego, CA 92198
www. ReferencePointPress.com

LIBRARY OF CONGRESS CATALOGING-IN-PUBLICATION DATA

Name: Hirschmann, Kris, 1967– author.
Title: Understanding Motivation / by Kris Hirschmann.
Description: San Diego, CA: ReferencePoint Press, [2018] | Series:
   Understanding Psychology | Audience: Grade 9 to 12. | Includes
   bibliographical references and index.
Identifiers: LCCN 2016059330 (print) | LCCN 2017016250 (ebook) | ISBN
   9781682822760 (eBook) | ISBN 9781682822753 (hardback)
Subjects: LCSH: Motivation (Psychology)—Juvenile literature. | Personality
   and motivation—Juvenile literature.
Classification: LCC BF503 (ebook) | LCC BF503 .H57 2018 (print) | DDC
   153.8—dc23
LC record available at https://lccn.loc.gov/2016059330

CONTENTS

The Human Brain: Thought, Behavior, and Emotion

Frontal lobe controls:
- Thinking
- Planning
- Organizing
- Problem solving
- Short-term memory
- Movement
- Personality
- Emotions
- Behavior
- Language

Parietal lobe:
- Interprets sensory information, such as taste, temperature, and touch

Temporal lobe:
- Processes information from the senses of smell, taste, and sound
- Plays role in memory storage

Occipital lobe:
- Processes images from the eyes
- Links information with images stored in memory

Source: Mayo Foundation for Education and Research, "Slide Show: How Your Brain Works." www.mayoclinic.org.

INTRODUCTION

What Is Motivation?

A man sits by himself in a quiet room. He is not watching TV, using a computer, listening to the radio, or receiving any type of input from the outside world. He is simply sitting there.

Suddenly, for no apparent reason, the man stands up. He stretches and looks around the room. He paces back and forth for a moment, then walks to the window. A smile appears on his face as he leans on the windowsill and gazes outside.

Why did the man do these things? Though an observer can guess at the reasons—perhaps the man was stiff or bored, heard a noise outside, or saw someone he knew—only the man himself knows for sure. One thing is certain, though: Something caused the man to spring into action. This something is known in psychological literature as motivation. In everyday language, it is why people do the things they do.

Defining Motivation

Motivation is the process that initiates, guides, and maintains goal-oriented behavior. Although motivation cannot be measured or quantified, it definitely exists—and by studying people's behavior, scientists can make guesses about the motivation behind those people's actions. As scientist Jeffrey S. Nevid explains, "We don't actually observe a motive; rather, we infer that one exists based on the behavior we observe."[1]

Psychologists have been trying to understand motivation in a more precise way since their field's earliest days. Many theories have been developed, and different views have been popular at different times. Today it is widely accepted that motivation involves a mix of biological, social, emotional, and cognitive factors. This mix is in constant flux, changing moment by moment relative to a person's body, mood, thoughts, and surroundings. As a result, a person's motivation—and ultimately his or her behavior—varies in unpredictable ways.

To complicate things even further, it is now understood that many behaviors are caused by mixed motives. In other words, a person can have many different reasons for doing something. An example is a male student who takes a bathroom break. The student's primary motivation is the physical need to urinate, but the fact that he seeks a restroom rather than a bush is motivated by social norms. His choice of the men's room instead of the women's room, too, is motivated by his desire to follow the social rules he has been taught. The student's ultimate behavior depends on all of these factors.

Components of Motivation

Whatever its source, motivation is known to have three main components. It consists of activation, which is the desire to initiate a behavior; persistence, which is continued effort toward a goal even though obstacles may exist; and intensity, which is the concentration and vigor applied toward achieving the goal.

Some goals are easy to achieve and require only a low level of motivation. If a woman realizes she has run out of milk, for instance, the need for milk activates a trip to the grocery store without much deep thought or evaluation. Upon arrival, the woman has to circle the parking lot a few times to find a spot—but she persists in the face of an easy obstacle. Inside the store, she is fully focused on buying milk and does not become distracted by the "buy one, get one free" piles of goods. In other words, she has sufficient intensity of motivation to get the job done.

For harder goals, a much higher level of motivation is needed in all three areas. For example, a high school student who is deciding whether or not to apply to college knows this pro-

> **WORDS IN CONTEXT**
>
> **motivation**
> The process that initiates, guides, and maintains goal-oriented behavior.

Some actions require more motivation to finish than others do. The process of applying to college, for example, is a complex one that a high school student must possess a great deal of motivation to complete.

cess will take great effort, so simply reaching the activation phase might take a lot of thought and soul searching. After activation, the student must show great persistence and intensity to walk through all the steps and obstacles of college application—taking the required tests, finding and printing out application forms, filling them out, assembling the required paperwork, preparing for alumni interviews, and so on. By starting and then continuing to tackle this daunting series of tasks, the student demonstrates a very high level of motivation.

Getting Things Done

Buying milk and applying to college are wildly different tasks. But they are alike in one key way: They either get done, or they do not. There is no in between. After all, people do not partly buy milk or partly get into college. They succeed, or they fail.

Motivation alone does not completely account for this outcome, of course. A person might be extremely motivated to buy milk and try very hard to achieve this goal—but if the world's dairies are on strike and no milk is available, he or she will still fail. On the flip side, a student might be very unmotivated to apply to college and might do a poor job on the application process—or even skip it altogether—yet still gain admission because his or her aunt happens to be the college president.

So it cannot quite be said that motivation is the key to success. But it would be fair to say that it is a major factor in most circumstances. Certainly, studying motivation can help explain why some people accomplish great things in life, while others never seem to get much done at all. By understanding the many factors that play a part in this difference, people can learn how to increase their own motivation levels—and in turn, how to maximize their chances of success.

CHAPTER 1

Theories of Motivation

In his book *Drive*, business motivation expert Daniel H. Pink describes the earliest history of human motivation, some fifty thousand years in the past. "We were trying to survive," he writes. "From roaming the savannah to gather food to scrambling for the bushes when a saber-toothed tiger approached, that drive guided most of our behavior. . . . It wasn't especially elegant, nor was it much different from those of rhesus monkeys, giant apes, or many other animals. But it served us nicely. It worked."[2]

But then, says Pink, something changed. People got smarter, and they formed more complex societies. At this point, he says, "an operating system based purely on the biological drive was inadequate. . . . And so in a feat of remarkable cultural engineering, we slowly replaced what we had with a version more compatible with how we'd begun working and living. . . . Humans are [now] more than the sum of our biological urges."[3]

This idea, though expressed by Pink in 2009, is not a new one. Psychologists have long agreed that while biology still motivates people in modern times, it is only one of many possible factors in human behavior. This basic idea, however, is where the agreement ends. Over the decades, different scientists have championed all sorts of theories about human motivation. A look at these theories reveals that there may be many reasons why people do the things they do.

Instinct Theory

The earliest theory of motivation focused on biological tendencies, also referred to as instincts. Psychologist William Mc-Dougall first proposed the instinct theory in the early 1900s.

McDougall defined instincts as goal-oriented behaviors that occur naturally and automatically in a species. In animals, instincts include behaviors such as migration and nest building. The animals do not have to learn these behaviors; they are born or hatched knowing how to do them. In humans examples include the rooting reflex, which is the tendency of newborns to move their head around and search for a nipple, and the maternal instinct, which is said to be an irresistible urge for mothers to protect their children.

McDougall studied people's actions to find as many examples as possible of inborn, automatic behavior. He eventually identified eighteen instincts—including comfort, hunger, curiosity, and sex—that he said motivated all human activity. Without these instincts, he said, people would simply stop functioning. "Take away these instinctive dispositions with their powerful impulses, and the organism would become incapable of activity of any kind; it would lie inert and motionless,"[4] he declared.

Some other scientists of the era agreed with McDougall's general idea, although their definitions of human instinct differed. William James, sometimes called the father of American psychology, came up with his own expanded list of thirty-seven instincts. Psychoanalyst Sigmund Freud took the opposite approach, boiling all instincts down to just two categories: actions related to survival (life) and those related to self-destruction (death). Everything people did, Freud said, was motivated by one of these two overarching goals.

Instinct theories of motivation were popular in their time, and there is no doubt that they do explain some aspects of human behavior. Today, though, psychologists feel that instinct theories are incomplete. They believe that humans are motivated by much more than mere biology. While instincts certainly should be considered, they cannot completely explain why people do the things they do.

Drive-Reduction Theory

Like the instinct theory, the drive-reduction theory of motivation focuses on biology. First proposed by psychologist Clark Hull in 1943, this theory suggests that people always seek to be in a state of internal balance, called homeostasis. This ideal state, however, can be disrupted by drives—needs that are either physical (such as thirst) or directly related to a physical need (such as the need for money to buy a beverage).

The disruption of homeostasis, says the drive-reduction theory, is very unpleasant. A person in a disrupted state is therefore highly motivated to correct the imbalance, and he or she will take action to solve the problem. A thirsty person, for example, might walk to the kitchen and drink a glass of water. If the person is out running errands, he or she might stop at a convenience store and buy a soda. Either way, the action is motivated by the drive of thirst. Once the imbalance is corrected, the motivation disappears, and the behavior stops.

Pioneering psychoanalyst Sigmund Freud (pictured) believed that all human behavior stems from one of only two instincts. These instincts are, according to his theory, actions related to survival and actions related to self-destruction.

The drive-reduction theory, like the instinct theory, seems to explain some aspects of human motivation. But it leaves many questions unanswered. For instance, it cannot account for the fact that people sometimes fast for days or even weeks to achieve a state of altered consciousness. Although these people must be extremely hungry, their physical need does not motivate them to eat; they resist this urge in order to pursue a different goal.

The drive-reduction theory also cannot explain actions that occur in the absence of physical drives. For example, someone who has just eaten dinner may unexpectedly land in a social situation in which food is being served. Although the person is not hungry at all, he or she might eat again just to be polite. This behavior may actually disrupt the person's homeostasis by resulting in a state of being uncomfortably full. But he or she does it anyway because in this situation, social norms are more motivating than physical needs.

Arousal Theory

Closely related to the drive-reduction theory, and developed around the same time, is the arousal theory of motivation. This theory also states that people are trying to achieve an internal balance. But the theory holds that rather than trying to reduce tension, as in the drive-reduction model, people are trying to achieve the perfect level of arousal (physical and mental stimulation). For example, a person whose arousal level drops too low might feel bored and might respond by going out to see a movie with friends. A person whose arousal level gets too high might leave a noisy party and go sit in a quiet place for a while.

The perfect level of arousal varies widely from person to person. Some people like high levels of arousal and constantly seek out stimulating environments. Photographer Bre Thurston places herself in this category. "I can't stand being bored so I take on a few too many things at once in order to stay busy, but I wouldn't have it any other way,"[5] she says.

Other people cannot tolerate heightened arousal states and feel strongly motivated to avoid them. In a 2013 article, actress Tina Lifford recalls a moment she felt this way. "I was in an argument with a boyfriend. He kept telling me he wasn't arguing, he was trying to have a conversation, [but] it made me uncomfortable. . . . I felt overwhelmed. . . . I jumped up and headed towards the bedroom door."[6] Lifford's urge to leave the room was an instinctive attempt to reduce a high and greatly uncomfortable arousal level.

As is true of all theories of motivation, the arousal theory seems to apply to some situations but not others. Psychologists agree that people do, in fact, have different optimal arousal levels and that they are motivated to find their perfect balance. However, the theory is compromised by the fact that people can overcome their natural tendencies.

The ending of Lifford's story is a case in point. The actress ultimately did not flee the conversation that was causing her so much emotional distress. Instead, she took a deep breath, stayed in the room, and struggled through the rest of the encounter. In other words, she chose to stay overstimulated—an outcome that contradicts the basic idea of the arousal theory.

Incentive Theory

By the mid- to late 1940s, it had become obvious that there were too many holes in the instinct, drive-reduction, and arousal theories of motivation. Psychologists started trying to plug these holes by adding new elements to the picture. One of these elements was the idea of incentives, or rewards for action. By introducing this concept, scientists hoped to explain why people's behavior was more than just the sum of their biological needs.

The incentive theory is straightforward. It states that a person will be motivated to do something if he or she gets a reward for this behavior. A reward can come in many forms. The delicious taste of a cookie, for example, is a reward for eating. A crisp twenty-dollar bill is a reward for mowing a neighbor's lawn. An approving smile and a "Well done" is a reward for meeting a parent's expectations.

WORDS IN CONTEXT

---

incentive
Something that motivates behavior. Incentives can be positive, such as rewards, or negative, such as punishments.

One strength of the incentive theory is that it takes individual differences into account. Not all people find the same things rewarding, and this fact helps explain why motivation varies so greatly from person to person. As psychologist Douglas Bernstein puts it, "Differences in behavior from one person to another or from one situation to another can be traced to the incentives available and the value a person places on those incentives at the time."[7]

The incentive theory also helps explain why the same person's motivation levels might change from one circumstance to another—it all depends on the size of the reward. A child who is offered one dollar to wash the family dog might feel unexcited about the chore and might even try to get out of doing it. But if the same child is offered one hundred dollars, the result will probably be very different. The incentive is high, and therefore the motivation is high as well.

Humanistic Theories

Although incentive theories provided some insight into human motivation, many psychologists felt that these theories were too narrow in scope. Key among this group was Abraham Maslow, who in 1943 proposed what is known as a humanistic theory of motivation. The word *humanistic* suggests that the theory focuses specifically on humans, with their unique needs and abilities, rather than on all organisms. In particular, a humanistic theory takes people's thoughts, intelligence, and reasoning abilities into account.

In Maslow's view, people have what he termed a hierarchy of needs. There are five levels in this hierarchy, which is usually depicted as a pyramid. At the base of the pyramid are the physiological needs for food, drink, sleep, warmth, and so on. The second level includes safety needs such as protection from the elements, order, stability, and freedom from fear. The third level includes needs for belonging, acceptance, emotional connection, and love. The fourth level includes what Maslow called esteem needs, such as the desire for independence, success, dominance, and self-respect. The fifth level makes up the tip of

Metamotivation

Long after psychologist Abraham Maslow introduced his famous hierarchy of needs, he continued to study the topic of human motivation. He eventually came to believe that there was a sixth level beyond his hierarchy. Maslow dubbed this level "metamotivation." This is a state in which a person no longer pursues selfish goals but rather is concerned with intrinsic values such as truth, beauty, goodness, excellence, simplicity, and so on. This state is possible only when all other lower-level needs have been met.

When Maslow was first developing this idea, he felt that intrinsic values were not included in humans' biological programming. He thought they developed only under particular, unusual circumstances and only for a small percentage of people. His use of the prefix *meta*, which means "beyond," reflected this idea: Metamotivation and metabeliefs were beyond what most people were capable of achieving.

Later in life, however, Maslow changed his mind. He came to believe that all people were in fact capable of this highest possible level of functioning. "The so-called spiritual . . . life is clearly rooted in the biological nature of the species," he wrote in 1971.

But the fact that metamotivation is possible for everyone does not mean it is common. This state is hard to reach and hard to maintain. Maslow believed only a small number of people would ever experience the ultimate level of human motivation.

Abraham H. Maslow, "The Good Life of the Self-Actualizing Person," in *Readings in Human Development: A Humanistic Approach*, ed. Theron M. Covin. New York: MSS Information Corporation, 1974, p. 53.

Self-actualization
morality, creativity, spontaneity, problem solving, lack of prejudice, acceptance of facts

Esteem
self-esteem, confidence, achievement, respect of others, respect by others

Love/belonging
friendship, family, sexual intimacy

Safety
security of: body, employment, resources, morality, the family, health, property

Physiological
breathing, food, water, sex, sleep, homeostasis, excretion

the pyramid and consists of needs related to self-actualization, or seeking growth and achieving one's full potential in life.

Maslow's theory states that people are motivated to pursue lower-level goals before higher-level goals. A person who is hungry, for example, will be motivated to find food before seeking satisfaction of needs that fall into levels two, three, four, and five. After the person eats, hunger ceases to be a motivator, and second-level goals become interesting. If the person satisfies all second-level needs, he or she moves up to the third level; when the third level is satisfied, the fourth level can be broached. Only after all of these levels have been conquered, says Maslow, will a person be motivated to tackle the fifth-level goals related to personal growth.

In a classic 1943 article, Maslow explained his thinking in terms that are easy to understand and accept. "A want that is satisfied is no longer a want. The organism is dominated and its behavior organized only by unsatisfied needs," he said. "If hunger is satisfied, it becomes unimportant in the current dynamics of the individual."[8] By using the term *current dynamics*, Maslow accounted for differences in motivation from one moment or circumstance to another.

ERG Theory

Maslow's hierarchy of needs went a long way toward explaining human motivation, and it has stood the test of time as an important psychological concept. It is still taught and used in various areas of study in the present day.

As it relates to motivation, however, Maslow's hierarchy has some shortcomings. In particular, critics feel that it does not account for the fact that people sometimes have several needs at once and may try to multitask in meeting them. For instance, a person who goes out to dinner with friends is meeting a level-one need for food and drink but simultaneously satisfying a level-three desire for social connection.

In 1969 psychologist Clayton Alderfer proposed a modified version of Maslow's hierarchy that addresses this problem by compressing Maslow's five levels into three: existence, relatedness, and growth (ERG). In the ERG model, the existence level forms the base of the pyramid and combines Maslow's levels one and two. Relatedness is the second level and includes Maslow's level three and some parts of level four. Growth is the tip of the pyramid and includes everything remaining.

Like Maslow's hierarchy, the ERG theory states that lower-level needs are more urgently motivating than higher-level needs. But Alderfer differs from Maslow by suggesting that needs from different levels can be motivating at the same time. He also acknowledges that needs vary based on the person, the circumstances, and even the time of life. For example, someone in his or her twenties may be motivated to go on lots of dates—but by the time the same person reaches his or her fifties, he or she might be much more interested in personal growth than romantic connection.

ERG theory also accounts for regression, or "backward progress." According to Alderfer, if higher-level needs are too hard to

Is Motivation Genetic?

Scientific studies suggest that many personality traits are programmed into people's genes. According to a 2015 paper, motivation is probably included in this group.

The paper in question is a twins study. Twins studies compare data from identical and fraternal (nonidentical) twins. Identical twins have the same genetic code, while fraternal twins do not. So if a study can show that identical twins are much more alike than fraternal twins in a certain way, the difference may have a biological basis.

The study authors summarized data from about thirteen thousand identical and nonidentical twins (about sixty-five hundred pairs in all) aged nine to sixteen years. They looked at two particular traits: the enjoyment of learning and self-perceived academic ability. Both of these traits had been shown in previous studies to affect motivation levels. The authors hoped to find evidence that identical twins tended to be alike in these ways.

Analysis of the data backed up this hypothesis. It showed that identical twins are in fact far more alike in their motivation levels than fraternal twins. This correlation held up across different academic subjects, ages, and cultures, suggesting that it is robust (scientifically strong). It seems that when it comes to motivation levels, the differences really might be written in our DNA.

meet, a person will become frustrated and unmotivated. He or she will go back to pursuing lower-level goals that have a greater chance of success.

Expectancy Theory

The idea of success is also important in the expectancy theory of motivation, first proposed by business school professor Victor Vroom in the mid-1960s. According to this theory, people think about the future and imagine what might happen if they do certain things. If a person expects a positive outcome, he or she will be highly motivated to pursue a goal. If the person expects a negative outcome, motivation levels will be much lower or nonexistent.

Vroom breaks motivation down into three key parts that he called valence, instrumentality, and expectancy. *Valence* refers to the value a person places on an outcome. *Instrumentality* refers to whether a person feels he or she has an important personal role to play in the outcome—in other words, whether the person is instrumental to a goal's success. *Expectancy* refers to a person's belief that he or she possesses the skills or knowledge to achieve the goal. The higher the valence, instrumentality, and expectancy of a goal, the more motivated a person will be to pursue it.

This theory can be understood through the example of a person with an engineering degree who is looking for a job and has the choice of applying for either Job 1, a well-paying engineering position, or Job 2, a low-paying construction job. The instrumentality of these goals is probably similar, but the valence and expectancy are much higher for the engineering job. Expectancy theory would therefore predict that this job hunter would be more motivated to apply for Job 1 than Job 2. However, the prediction might change if the job hunter were a construction worker or if the pay scales of the two jobs were reversed.

The Right Combination

All of the theories of motivation describe some aspects of human motivation. But psychologists agree that no single theory can completely explain why people do the things they do. Humans are complex and are motivated by different things at different times. The trick is finding the right combination of motivations, at the right times and under the right circumstances, to inspire goal-oriented behavior—and ultimately to lead to the desired result.

Motivation from Without and Within

A student sets his alarm clock for 6:00 a.m. every school morning. When the alarm goes off, he drags himself out of bed and starts to get ready. He is not an early riser by nature, and he often wishes he could stay in bed. But he knows he will get in trouble if he is tardy, so he resists the temptation. He does the things he must do to get to school on time.

One Saturday morning, his alarm goes off at 6:00 a.m. as usual. This time the youth flies out of bed. He is going to run a 5K race with a friend, and he feels excited and happy. He gets ready with a bounce in his step and a smile on his face, and he is out the door in record time.

In these examples, the youth is motivated to do the identical thing—setting his alarm clock and getting up early—for two different reasons. In the first example, he gets up because he has to. This is an example of motivation from without, also called extrinsic motivation. In the second example, he gets up because he wants to. This is an example of motivation from within, also called intrinsic motivation. Both kinds of motivation influence human behavior.

Seeking Rewards

Rewards provide the most basic type of extrinsic motivation. A reward is anything positive that a person receives in exchange for performing a certain action.

Some rewards are material, which means they are actual items of value. Examples of material rewards include cash, prizes, coupons for free goods or services, points on a credit card, and so on—the list is endless. One very common type of material reward is a salary. A person is hired for a job that requires him or her to handle a specific list of duties, usually during a fixed time period (such as 9:00 a.m. to 5:00 p.m., Monday through Friday). The person receives the reward of money in return for meeting these obligations.

Sometimes rewards are emotional instead of material. An emotional reward is one that simply makes a person feel good. Examples include praise, applause, increased privileges, and other similar positive things. This type of reward might be used, for instance, to toilet train a child. Each time the child successfully uses the toilet, he or she gets lots of hugs, kisses, and praise from the happy parents. The child finds this attention very motivating and will perform to receive it.

Material and emotional rewards can both be effective, depending on the person and the circumstances. They can also be combined. In the toilet-training example, for instance, the parents might decide to give the child a small piece of candy along with praise. They are trying to find the right balance of rewards to motivate their child.

Avoiding Punishment

While rewards motivate people to do something, an extrinsic motivator called punishment does exactly the opposite: It motivates people not to do something. There are two types of punishment: positive punishment (when something undesired is added) and negative punishment (when a desired item or privilege is removed).

The difference between the two types of punishment can be illustrated through the example of a teenager who is rude to a teacher. The teen receives detention as a consequence for her behavior. The teen's offended teacher also forces her to write an essay about respecting authority. Both of these consequences are positive punishments because they add unpleasant things to the teen's

> **WORDS IN CONTEXT**
>
> **extrinsic**
> Originating from without; arising from positive or negative influences in a person's environment.

Some actions are motivated by what people feel they have to do, while others are motivated by what people want to do. For example, people participating in a competition such as a marathon generally do so because they want to, rather than because they must.

day: She must attend detention, and she must write a boring essay.

Later in the day, the same unruly teen arrives home. Her parents have heard from the school's principal and, furious, decide to impose their own punishment on their daughter. They take away her cell phone for a week, and they ground her. These consequences are negative punishments because the parents are taking privileges away. By imposing them, the parents hope to motivate their daughter to behave better in the future.

Who Cares?

Extrinsic motivation, both positive and negative, has a long track record of success in getting people to do things, and the results of this type of motivation are fairly predictable. Daniel H. Pink sums up the basic concept nicely when he explains, "Rewarding an activity will get you more of it. Punishing an activity will get you less of it."[9]

This approach is so successful, in fact, that it can motivate people to behave in ways that do not match up with their interests. They will tolerate a boring task if they think the reward will make it all worthwhile. As one scientist puts it, "An extrinsically motivated person will work on a task even when they have little interest in it because of the anticipated satisfaction they will get from some reward."[10] Conversely, a person will avoid something enjoyable if he or she thinks the punishment will outweigh any pleasure that might result.

Examples of this behavior abound in the everyday world. A student who hates math, for instance, will do all assigned math homework to earn an A in the class. An employee who dislikes a job will show up on time every day and slog through the work to earn a regular paycheck. A driver who loves going fast will stick to the speed limit to avoid getting an expensive ticket. If the extrinsic motivators were removed, however, the picture would change completely. The student would skip the math homework, the employee would quit the job, and the driver would speed up. Without any hope of a reward or threat of punishment, there is no longer any motivation to perform the tasks, so the behavior disappears.

> **WORDS IN CONTEXT**
>
> **reward**
> Something positive a person receives, either material or emotional, in return for a behavior.

Biological Drives

The situation is quite different with regard to biological needs, the most basic of the intrinsic motivators. These are usually called drives. They include needs for food, drink, sleep, oxygen, and sexual satisfaction. Since physical drives are related to an organism's survival, they can be overwhelmingly strong. A person will be highly motivated to satisfy them even in the absence of external incentives.

Drives are such a natural part of being human that we do not think much about them under normal circumstances. During a typical day, most people will have moments of feeling hungry, thirsty, sleepy, hot, cold, and so on. Usually, the person who feels these things will simply take care of them with very little thought: He or she will eat, drink, sleep, and remove or add a jacket. These needs are expected, so they do not worry the person, who is automatically motivated to take care of them before becoming too uncomfortable.

If for some reason people cannot satisfy their drives quickly, they start to feel progressively higher levels of physical distress. As the drive increases, the person's motivation to reduce the drive also increases, to the point that the person will do practically anything to bring his or her body back into balance.

This fact lies behind some interrogation techniques. In the technique of sleep deprivation, for example, prisoners are not permitted to sleep for days on end. Their discomfort becomes so acute that they will do or say whatever their captors tell them to end it. In his memoirs, former Israeli prime minister Menachem Begin describes this state. "In the head of the interrogated prisoner a haze begins to form. His spirit is wearied to death, his legs are unsteady, and he has one sole desire: to sleep, to sleep just a little, not to get up, to lie, to rest, to forget. . . . Anyone who has experienced this desire knows that not even hunger or thirst are comparable with it,"[11] he writes.

The Curious Case of Harlow's Monkeys

Until the mid-1900s, psychologists believed that some combination of rewards, punishments, and drives motivated all behavior.

26

Negative punishments occur when a desired item or privilege is removed, such as a parent taking away a teen's mobile phone privileges. Positive punishments, by contrast, occur when something undesired is given, such as a teen being assigned extra household chores.

But that thinking was challenged in 1949 by scientist Harry F. Harlow, who accidentally discovered something that called the accepted view of motivation into question.

The discovery came during an experiment in which Harlow gave simple puzzles to eight rhesus monkeys. To solve the puzzles, the monkeys had to manipulate pins, hooks, and hinges in the right order. Harlow's original goal was to train the monkeys to do these puzzles. He gave the items to the monkeys before the training began to let them become familiar with each item. Harlow expected the monkeys to examine the puzzles briefly, then ignore them. But much to his surprise, the monkeys started playing with the puzzles and quickly learned how to solve them—and they did this with no training, rewards, or punishment whatsoever.

This behavior should not have been possible, according to then-current theories of motivation. Yet it had happened. The only explanation, said Harlow, was that "the performance of the task provided intrinsic reward."[12] In other words, the monkeys solved the puzzles simply because they enjoyed it, and that pleasure was rewarding enough to create motivation.

Much has been learned about intrinsic rewards since Harlow's groundbreaking discovery. Today psychologists understand that this type of motivation drives a great deal of human behavior. It comes into play in many different areas of people's lives.

Just for Fun

The desire for fun is one such area. Psychologists agree that people are naturally wired to need play and enjoyment, and they are motivated to do things that satisfy this need.

It is easiest to see this tendency in children. Young boys and girls are endlessly playful, and they do not need to be rewarded

Operant Conditioning

A concept called operant conditioning is closely related to motivation. The theory of operant conditioning states that people and animals can be trained to respond in certain ways via external stimuli. In other words, they will be motivated to do specific things under specific circumstances.

Psychologist B.F. Skinner famously explored this idea in the early 1930s with a series of experiments. He invented a small chamber that could hold rats, flies, and other subjects in a highly controlled environment. Skinner then introduced rewards (such as food) or punishments (such as heat). By consistently rewarding some behaviors while punishing others, Skinner trained the animals to respond to stimuli in predictable ways.

Skinner's experiments reveal an interesting overlap between voluntary and involuntary behavior. He showed that while organisms do have the ability to choose their responses, the "right" choice can become so deeply ingrained that it is virtually guaranteed. By using the techniques of operant conditioning, Skinner shaped his subjects' motivations to match his desired outcomes.

or prompted to engage in this behavior. "Do you remember how awesome it was to be a kid?" one blogger wistfully recalls. "Every day was a new opportunity to play, every person was a potential playmate, and every household item had the ability to be turned into something cool and fun, like a few blankets and chairs becoming a secret fort."[13]

Adults tend to be less playful than children. They have more responsibilities in life, and these responsibilities can conflict with the desire to play. But adults still do many things just for fun. For instance, an avid reader devours novels for the pleasure of the stories, not for any extrinsic reward. A baker concocts delicious treats in the kitchen simply because he loves to cook. A knitter spends weeks handcrafting a sweater because she finds the process relaxing. Or a person goes to extreme lengths and expense to decorate for the holidays, just because he or she enjoys it. "It takes about three days to put up," says one homeowner of her epic Halloween display. "I do it just for fun. . . . It's fun to build the stuff."[14]

Very Curious

Related to fun is the feeling of curiosity, another intrinsic motivator. Curiosity is a strong desire to know or learn something. This feeling motivates a person to behave in ways that provide answers.

There are two types of curiosity, identified by psychologist Daniel Berlyne in the mid-1900s. The first, called specific curiosity, Berlyne defined as "a tendency to investigate a specific object or problem in order to understand it."[15] An example of this type of curiosity would be the desire to visit a new store. A person sees the new building going up and wonders what goods the store carries. These thoughts create motivation to patronize the new establishment.

The second type of curiosity is called diversive curiosity. Berlyne defined it as "a general tendency for a person to seek novelty, take risks, and search for adventure."[16] A person who loves traveling to foreign countries is demonstrating this type of curiosity. He or she feels curious about the world and wants to see as much of it as possible. The motivation created by this feeling is so strong that the person may spend considerable time, effort, and money to satisfy it.

Psychologists point out that a person's level of curiosity is directly related to his or her motivation. If the curiosity is low, the motivation to explore is also low or even nonexistent. As the level of curiosity goes up, a person's motivation level also increases, and curiosity-satisfying behavior is more likely to occur.

I Can Do It

The feeling of challenge is yet another intrinsic motivator that can drive people's behavior. Challenge is the desire to achieve something difficult without hope or expectation of external rewards. Personal satisfaction is the only goal.

There are almost limitless levels of challenge. At a low level, for example, a toddler struggles to learn how to tie his or her shoes, just to feel the thrill of accomplishment. At a somewhat higher level, a teen spends hours playing a favorite video game to reach ever-higher rankings.

Near the top of the scale are the extreme physical challenges that require people to push themselves to their limits. A recreational runner might decide, for example, to try to qualify for a marathon. To achieve this goal, the runner must adopt a grueling training schedule and follow it for months. If the race is in another city, he or she may also have to save enough money to pay for an airplane ticket and a hotel room for the weekend of the race. His or her desire for a challenge is strong enough to motivate these behaviors, even though the only reward will be a feeling of personal accomplishment.

One avid mountain climber puts this feeling into words when explaining his motivation to climb Mount Everest, the world's highest peak. "The drive comes from my own desire to challenge myself and to explore what is *new to me*. . . . The experience of a summit, even on routine climbs, rivals anything else I've done. It is my rush,"[17] he explains.

Mixed Motivation

While these examples depict situations in which the motivations are simple and clear-cut, in real life the picture is often much more

Conquering Mount Everest (pictured) is a goal shared by many mountain climbers. Even though the only reward will be a feeling of personal accomplishment, these climbers are motivated by the desire for a challenge.

complex. It is not only possible but common for people to have mixed motivations for the things they do.

A professional football player, for example, might have grown up loving football and seeking every possible opportunity to play the game, doing so only for enjoyment—in other words, he had an intrinsic love of the game. As an adult, this player still has that intrinsic love and relishes every moment on the field. But as a professional, he also receives extrinsic rewards in the form of money, fame, and cheering crowds. He is now motivated by more than simply his love of the game.

Another complicating factor when considering motivation is that a given behavior can be motivated either intrinsically or extrinsically, depending on the situation. Eating habits may be the most studied example of this puzzle. A person might eat due to intrinsic motivations such as hunger, boredom, stress, or habit. He or she might also eat due to extrinsic motivations such as

Sixteen Basic Desires

In a 1998 study of six thousand people, scientist Steven Reiss found sixteen basic needs, values, and desires that he claims motivate nearly all human behavior. Reiss's list comprises the following:

- Acceptance, the need to be appreciated

- Curiosity, the need to gain knowledge

- Eating, the need for food

- Family, the need to take care of one's offspring

- Honor, the need to be faithful to the customary values of an individual's ethnic group, family, or clan

- Idealism, the need for social justice

- Independence, the need to be distinct and self-reliant

- Order, the need for prepared, established, and conventional environments

- Physical activity, the need for movement of the body

- Power, the need for control of will

- Romance, the need for mating or sex

- Saving, the need to accumulate something

- Social contact, the need for relationship with others

- Social status, the need for social significance

- Tranquility, the need to be secure and protected

- Vengeance, the need to strike back against another person

To measure these desires, Reiss devised a test called the Reiss Motivation Profile that measures a person's level in each area. The test reveals differences between people and helps shed light on the often confusing subject of human motivation.

familial or social pressure. To an observer, the end behavior is identical: Food gets eaten. But the internal state that causes the behavior—the motivation—is not clear to anyone other than the person doing the eating.

A Complicated Picture

Studies show clearly that intrinsic motivation is usually more effective than extrinsic motivation. People who do something because they want to will almost always be more motivated than those who do something because they have to.

Beyond that truth, however, it becomes very tricky to identify people's motivations. Human behavior is caused by different things at different times, and it depends on an ever-changing balance of intrinsic and extrinsic motivators. The best way to summarize this situation is perhaps unsatisfying but ultimately true: It is complicated.

The Reward Dilemma

A young woman spends one day a month volunteering for her favorite charity. She does not receive or expect any payment for her time. She volunteers because she likes the work and thinks it is important. She is intrinsically motivated to be involved.

But one day something changes. The charity's leaders decide to give its volunteers ten dollars per day. They do this partly because they want to show their appreciation to hardworking helpers. They also hope the money will be a small incentive to keep volunteers coming back. In other words, they hope that it will provide some added extrinsic motivation.

Instead of being more motivated, however, the young woman starts to feel just the opposite. Although she understands the ten dollars is not meant to be a salary, she still feels annoyed that the charity places so little value on her time. Her motivation plummets, and she becomes less and less interested in volunteering. After a few months, she stops doing so altogether.

This story illustrates the tricky balancing act between rewards and motivation. Rewards do motivate people—sometimes. But at other times, they have exactly the opposite effect. Psychologists today are working hard to understand this relationship since it applies to many areas of human behavior.

Carrots and Sticks

Any discussion of the reward dilemma centers on the concept of "carrots and sticks," a phrase that is commonly used in motivation literature. This phrase refers to rewards and punishments, which are the two types of extrinsic motivators. The phrase can be understood by imagining a person trying to coax an ornery horse across a field. The person can motivate the animal by tempting it with a tasty carrot (a reward), by driving it forward with blows from a stick (a punishment), or by some combination of the two.

Literal carrots and sticks are seldom used to motivate people. But on a metaphorical level, the concept remains the same. Anything that rewards a person is a carrot. Anything that punishes a person is a stick. By applying these things, the theory holds, motivation will be created, and a desired behavior will occur.

There are countless examples of carrots and sticks in everyday life. In the business world, for example, one common carrot is the performance bonus. This is a sum of money, separate from a salary, that employees can earn if they perform at an exceptional level. Management hopes the bonus will motivate employees to go above and beyond their regular job duties.

> **WORDS IN CONTEXT**
>
> **carrot**
>
> A material reward that can be earned by performing a certain task.

A familiar example of a stick occurs in high school and college sports, in which athletes are usually required to maintain a minimum grade point average (GPA). If an athlete's GPA falls below the minimum, the athlete is suspended from the team until the GPA rebounds. This punishment is a stick that is used to motivate academic effort.

Harlow's Monkeys, Part Two

Carrots and sticks were long thought to have a precise, almost mathematical effect on human behavior. This principle, however, was called into question by Harlow's monkeys—the same ones that surprised researchers by demonstrating intrinsic motivation to do puzzles. In a further development, Harlow thought the monkeys would be even more motivated if he rewarded them, so he started giving them raisins each time they solved a puzzle. Much to Harlow's surprise, the raisins did not improve the monkeys' performance; the animals actually started making more mistakes and solving the puzzles less frequently than before. In other words, they were less motivated, not more.

Psychologists of the day did not know what to make of this result, so it went mostly unstudied for a long time. But decades later, another scientist named Edward Deci decided to take a deeper look. In 1969 he devised a study that, like Harlow's experiment, asked subjects to solve puzzles. This time the subjects were human, but the results were exactly the same: Motivation levels were highest when the subjects got no reward, and they dropped when rewards were introduced. Based on this result, Deci reached the conclusion that material rewards could actually hurt performance. "When money is used as an external reward for some activity, the subjects lose intrinsic interest,"[18] he stated.

WORDS IN CONTEXT

---

stick

A punishment that will occur if a certain task is not performed.

The Overjustification Effect

This finding was controversial in Deci's day because it flew against the conventional wisdom of the time. However, over subsequent years, this result was repeated in multiple experiments, until the psychology community finally had no choice but to accept it. The phenomenon became known as the overjustification effect. Today scientists understand that this concept holds true for many types of extrinsic rewards.

Many theories have been put forward to explain the overjustification effect. One well-known theory suggests that when people are rewarded for doing something, they tend to focus on the reward rather than on any intrinsic pleasure they get from the task. The task therefore becomes less enjoyable, and motivation decreases accordingly.

Another theory suggests that people may feel pushed or forced by rewards. In other words, they may want to do something just for the enjoyment of it—but if someone then offers a tangible reward, it seems like a sort of bribe. This pressure can be

People often are motivated to do work such as volunteering at an animal shelter with no expectation of a reward. In fact, in some cases rewards can decrease their motivation to do so, illustrating the tricky balance that exists between rewards and motivation.

annoying and cause someone to lose all motivation to behave in the desired way.

A feeling of getting shortchanged may be yet another reason for the overjustification effect. If a reward is too small for the perceived amount of work, people may feel irritated, as if someone is trying to take advantage of them. This creates a negative attitude and a lack of motivation, and it may ultimately lead to a refusal to continue the activity at any level.

Rewards for Creativity

The overjustification effect has a severely negative impact on motivation. It has been shown to be particularly harmful to creative activities such as artistic work and play.

Professor Teresa Amabile of Harvard Business School is one of the foremost researchers in this area. In the 1990s Amabile and her colleagues studied the relationship between creativity and the overjustification effect by showing 460 paintings to a group of experts. Some of the paintings were commissioned pieces, which means they were ordered and paid for in advance, and the artists were required to follow a series of instructions or guidelines. The rest of the paintings were noncommissioned, which means the artists created them for no one in particular, with no rules to follow. The experts consistently rated the noncommissioned paintings as being more creative than those done for clients.

The comments of a professional artist who does both commissioned and noncommissioned work shed some light on this result. "Not always, but a lot of the time, when you are doing a piece for someone else it becomes more 'work' than joy," she explains. "When I work for myself there is the pure joy of creating and I can work through the night and not even know it. On a commissioned piece you have to check yourself—be careful to do what the client wants."[19]

In Amabile's study, extrinsic rewards did not erase the artists' motivation. The commissioned pieces were completed. But they did not get done as well—or at least as creatively—as they might have under different circumstances. By focusing on extrinsic rewards, the artists replaced their naturally joyful motivation with a desire to conform to a standard, and their performance suffered as a result.

Rewards for Doing Good

The desire to do good deeds is another area in which material rewards sometimes do more harm than good. People who are motivated by feelings of altruism might do many things—such as donating money, time, goods, or services—merely because they think they should. They get a warm, satisfied feeling from their actions, arising from the conviction that they are good people

Schools Without Grades

Basic education is a long and difficult process. It takes twelve to thirteen years and requires huge amounts of time and effort. Yet in America, at least, studies show that the education system as it currently stands does not intrinsically motivate the majority of students. Most do their work because of carrots and sticks, and many do only the bare minimum required to get by.

To correct this problem, some schools are turning to a system called competency-based education. In a competency-based system, students are required to learn certain skills and facts to progress. They must demonstrate their mastery of these things to move to the next level. But it is all done without grades, awards, or other similar extrinsic motivators.

Critics of competency-based education worry that without grades, students will never develop the grit they need to compete in the adult world. But supporters claim that the truth is exactly the reverse. "The best [competency-based] schools today are great because they reach the students who appeared to be 'unmotivated' in the old system. . . . Students only progress once they have truly mastered a concept, not based on time," explains one expert. By removing extrinsic rewards, these programs may actually increase motivation by putting intrinsic factors back into the picture.

Michael Horn, "Building Motivation, Instilling Grit: The Necessity of Mastery-Based, Digital Learning," *Forbes*, January 10, 2013. www.forbes.com.

doing the right thing. This feeling is the only reward they need to be intrinsically motivated.

Adding extrinsic rewards in these cases seems as if it should increase motivation even further. But like the raisins given to Harlow's monkeys, material rewards actually seem to decrease the motivation for altruistic actions. One study suggests, for example, that small payments make regular blood donors less likely to donate. The author of that study speculates that the reward overshadows the original motivation, which in turn makes the activity less appealing.

In another study, researchers pretended to accidentally drop objects, then asked toddlers to retrieve them. Some of the toddlers received rewards for doing this good deed, while others did not. After a number of trials, the researchers stopped the rewards but continued to drop objects. The toddlers who had never been rewarded kept right on being helpful. Most of the previously rewarded toddlers, on the other hand, lost interest in helping out. "Rewarding children for altruistic behavior causes them to be less likely to be altruistic in the future,"[20] the study's authors concluded.

Rewards Are Addictive

This study highlights another important problem with material rewards: They have an addictive effect. Once they are provided, it is nearly impossible to remove them without destroying a person's motivation, as shown by the behavior of the toddlers in the study.

Another example of this principle would be the case of a teen who occasionally pet-sits for a neighboring family. At first the teen does this just for a day or two here and there. It is not much trouble, and no money changes hands. But when the family plans a weeklong vacation, the parents feel uncomfortable asking for such a big favor, so they offer payment in return for the pet-sitting service. From this point forward, the teen will expect to be paid, regardless of the number of days involved. He or she will feel very unmotivated to help without this reward.

In such a case, the standard payment will probably continue to get the job done over subsequent occasions. In other situations, however, the reward—like any other addictive thing—must be increased over time to remain effective. As one writer explains it, "Cash rewards and shiny trophies can provide a delicious jolt of pleasure at first, but the feeling soon dissipates—and to keep it alive, the recipient requires ever larger and more frequent doses."[21] One example would be a student athlete who is thrilled with the first ribbon he or she earns at a swim meet. A year or two down the road, though, the same athlete may have earned a dozen ribbons, so that type of reward has become much less exciting. Now the athlete wants a trophy, and no smaller reward will satisfy or motivate him or her.

Cutting Corners

These examples show how material rewards can reduce or destroy motivation. These effects are an important part of the reward dilemma—but the problems do not stop there. Another serious concern is that rewards can motivate people in the wrong ways, leading them to cut corners or cheat to accomplish tasks.

In 2016 a scandal involving the Wells Fargo financial institution provided a shocking illustration of this effect. Regulators discovered that thousands of Wells Fargo employees had been opening fake accounts without customers' permission. They did this

In 2016, news reports revealed that employees of the Wells Fargo financial institution were engaging in shady practices by opening new accounts without customers' knowledge or permission. The combination of big rewards for success and the punishment of losing their jobs for failure was the motivation for the employees' behavior.

because the company paid its employees poorly but offered them big bonuses—carrots—for selling new accounts. At the same time, employees were told they could lose their jobs—sticks—if they did not perform. "I was always getting written up for failing to bump my . . . numbers up,"[22] recalls one former employee.

With this combination of rewards and punishment, Wells Fargo undoubtedly hoped to foster a demanding but exciting environment in which the best employees would be highly motivated to shine. Instead, the company created a situation that motivated employees to cut corners and find illegal solutions. It is one of the highest-profile examples of motivation gone wrong to hit the newsstands in recent years. As such, the Wells Fargo situation serves as a cautionary tale about the perils of rewards and punishments.

Meeting the Minimum

It is clear that material rewards can be counterproductive and even damaging to motivation. One might wonder, therefore, why they are even used at all. But it turns out that there are some situations in which material rewards are vital for motivation.

One of these situations was addressed by psychologist Frederick Herzberg with his hygiene-motivation theory, also known as the two-factor theory. This theory states in part that a job must provide certain baseline rewards, or hygiene factors, before an employee will perform in any way at all. Hygiene factors include things such as a fair salary and benefits, a safe and comfortable working environment, and reasonable interpersonal relationships with coworkers. Since these minimum rewards must be met to prevent employees from being dissatisfied and unmotivated, providing them is a clear necessity and can only help, not harm, motivation levels. The same holds true in non-work-related environments such as education, sports, and countless other areas.

Another situation in which rewards become essential is when routine, nonintrinsically motivating tasks must be accomplished. An example would be working on an assembly line. This type of work is boring, mindless, and noncreative. People generally have no intrinsic motivation to perform it. Extrinsic motivation such as

Tom Sawyer's Fence

In the early pages of the book *The Adventures of Tom Sawyer* by Mark Twain, the title character is sent by his aunt to whitewash a wooden fence. The task is dull and holds no intrinsic interest for Tom whatsoever, and he approaches it with reluctance: "He surveyed the fence, and all gladness left him and a deep melancholy settled down upon his spirit. Thirty yards of board fence nine feet high. Life to him seemed hollow, and existence but a burden."

In his misery, Tom considers bribing his friends to do the work for him. He checks his pockets, which contain a variety of small items, but finds nothing with any motivational value: "Not half enough to buy so much as half an hour of pure freedom. So he returned his straitened means to his pocket, and gave up the idea of trying to buy the boys."

But then Tom hits on an idea. Instead of using material rewards—carrots—to tempt his friends, he decides to give the whitewashing job intrinsic appeal by saying it is too hard for them. Tom's friends feel challenged by this statement, and they decide that they desperately want to whitewash the fence. They even end up paying Tom for the privilege. Tom ends the day with his pockets jammed full of little treasures, musing on the lesson he has learned: "Work consists of whatever a body is *obliged* to do, and Play consists of whatever a body is not obliged to do." By finding the right reward, Tom motivates his friends to fulfill his wishes.

Mark Twain, *The Adventures of Tom Sawyer*. Hartford, CT: American, 1884. www.projectgutenberg.com.

generous salaries and production bonuses therefore provide the best—and perhaps the only—chance of getting the desired results.

The Right Way to Reward

The growing realization that rewards can hurt motivation creates a dilemma for organizations in multiple fields. Businesses, schools, governments, and other entities must motivate their employees and populations if they wish to succeed. If carrots and sticks do not work, then what does?

There is no one-size-fits-all answer to this question, but psychologists have learned a few helpful things. One is that surprise rewards are not as harmful as expected rewards. This means, for instance, that a manager can safely hand an employee a $500 check for doing an outstanding job or a softball coach can surprise players with a pizza party after a big game. As long as the employee does not expect the check or the players do not expect the pizza, everyone will be delighted and happy. There will be no ill effects on the reward recipients' future motivation.

Using intangible rather than material rewards also seems to be a good strategy. Intangible rewards might include praise and positive feedback. People tend to love these rewards and find them extremely motivating, and such rewards never get old—in fact, it is just the opposite. Most people cannot get enough of them. Working on this principle, a teacher might take a student aside and praise him or her privately for an especially good science fair project. These kind words, which take no work at all and only seconds of the teacher's time, are likely to motivate the student more than an A+ with no personal recognition.

These types of rewards are not carrots, because they are given freely and are not tied to performance. Any motivation they create will be in the future, not the present. For this reason, they are often neglected in the day-to-day rush for accomplishment. Smart organizations, though, find ways to work them into their procedures. By choosing rewards that work rather than the traditional carrots and sticks, organizations just might be able to dodge the reward dilemma.

CHAPTER 4

Getting and Staying Motivated

Psychologists know that some people seem to be endlessly motivated, while others are not. Two high school students provide an example. One, who earns mostly Bs and Cs in his classes, feels disappointed in himself whenever he gets his report card. He knows that grades are important, and he admires his friends who work hard and receive top grades. He feels sure that he could do better, too, if he put in the time and effort. But he cannot seem to find the motivation. By contrast, his classmate earns mostly A's. This is not always easy; some of the classes are difficult, and sometimes she feels discouraged. But whenever this happens, she gives herself a pep talk and tries even harder. She stays motivated to do her best work, even during challenging situations.

The differences illustrated by these examples are quite common. The good news for people who struggle with motivation is that this state can be changed. Psychologists have learned that there are many practical ways to get and stay motivated.

Seek Opportunities

Opportunity is the most basic building block of motivation. Without it, motivation is unlikely to exist at all, and even if it does, it cannot produce any results. For example, a man who has no gym membership or gym access is unlikely to feel motivated to go to the gym. If for some reason he does feel that way—perhaps, for instance, he sees a fitness show on TV that inspires him—he still cannot act on that motivation because he does not have the opportunity. If the man subsequently goes out and joins a gym, however, he creates a situation in which motivation can lead to action.

Another example is a stay-at-home mother who wants to reenter the workforce. Because she spends her days at home with her children, she has little opportunity to network and learn about job openings. She feels confused and uncertain about what to do, which causes her to feel unmotivated to look for a job. If she gets out of the house and starts to meet new people, however, or perhaps attends a job fair, she will open herself to new opportunities. One of those opportunities might sound exciting, and this in turn might motivate the woman to put in a job application.

Choose Appropriate Targets

Once an opportunity exists, the next step to building motivation is to choose appropriate targets. Studies show clearly that people are highly motivated by tasks of medium difficulty. This means the tasks are hard enough to be challenging but easy enough to be manageable. One scientist sums up this concept in a way that most people can relate to:

> When facing a task, which do you find more motivating—doing something easy that you've done a hundred times and could probably do in your sleep, or doing something that is within the realm of possibilities but requires learning something new or stretching your existing abilities? For many people, the first option might be the easiest, but the second more challenging option will probably sound more interesting and motivating.[23]

A familiar example from everyday life is a science fair project. A student might feel bored by a very simple topic but overwhelmed by a very difficult one. His or her motivation will suffer in both cases. A student who chooses a challenging but interesting and achievable topic, on the other hand, is likely to feel much more motivated to do his or her best work. Aiming toward the middle gives the student the best possible chance of success.

Set Goals

Once the feeling of motivation exists, goals can help people stay on track and prevent their motivation from disappearing. Goal setting has become a popular subject in recent decades, and a great deal of advice has been set forth by experts in many different fields.

One of the best-known and most often repeated statements is that goals should be SMART. This is an acronym that stands for specific, measurable, attainable, realistic, and timely. The first two words, *specific* and *measurable*, go hand in hand and mean that goals must be phrased in a way that is crystal clear and concrete. *Attainable* and *realistic* are also related and mean that goals must actually be achievable and reasonable. The final word, *timely*, means that a goal should have a clear timeline.

A personal goal such as eating more fresh fruits and vegetables is more likely to be achieved if the goal is SMART—specific, measurable, attainable, realistic, and timely—than if it is not.

This concept can be illustrated with the example of a person who wants to improve his or her health. This person might say to friends and family, "My goal is to get healthier." While the person's intentions are good, this statement is vague and does not really explain what the person wants to do. A SMART statement would sound more like, "I will begin eating a twelve-hundred-calorie-per-day diet and work out four days per week for thirty minutes each time. I will stick to this plan for ninety days, then evaluate my progress and set a new goal." Clear and specific, this goal lays out a plan of action that is easy to follow—and therefore motivational.

Simplicity is not the only reason a SMART goal improves motivation. Psychologists also point out that effective goals cut through the confusing clutter of everyday life and provide a path of action. As one writer puts it, "Goal setting is powerful because it provides focus. It shapes our dreams. It gives us the ability to hone in on the exact actions we need to perform to achieve everything we desire in life."[24] By boiling big dreams down to their simplest steps, goals encourage people to believe that they can and will succeed—and this belief, in turn, acts as a powerful motivator.

Stay in Control

The feeling of autonomy has been proved to be another powerful motivator. Autonomy is the ability to make choices according to one's free will. In any given situation, a person who feels this type of personal power tends to be highly motivated. A person who lacks this feeling, on the other hand, often loses motivation to cooperate and may even start to fight the task at hand. "If my wife tells me to do something I like—exercise, for example—I resent it and will actually want to resist doing it in order to preserve my sense of autonomy,"[25] says one man.

A 2006 study underscored the power of autonomy in the business world. Researchers studied 320 small businesses that used

Self-Determination Theory

A psychological construct called self-determination theory is one well-known effort to explain how people become and stay motivated. Psychologists Edward Deci and Richard Ryan, who developed the theory, suggest that people are driven by a need to grow personally and obtain fulfillment. They believe that this drive is intrinsic and natural to all people. They feel that without mastering challenges and having new experiences, a person cannot develop a cohesive sense of self.

Although the need for personal growth is ingrained, it must be actively pursued. Self-determination theory says that to exercise this drive, people need to feel three things:

- **Competence.** Competence is the mastery of tasks and skills.

- **Autonomy.** Autonomy is the feeling of control over one's own goals and actions.

- **Relatedness.** Relatedness is a sense of belonging and attachment to other people.

When these three universal needs are satisfied, say Deci and Ryan, people feel motivated, productive, and happy. When these needs are not satisfied, motivation plummets. By taking these aspects of self-determination theory into account, organizations and individuals can ensure that the baseline conditions for motivation are in place.

different models of management. Half of the businesses used traditional models in which employees were told exactly what to do and how to do it. The other half let employees decide for themselves how to do their jobs. The results were striking. The businesses that offered autonomy grew at four times the rate of the control-oriented firms. They also had one-third the amount of turnover (employees quitting and needing to be replaced). From these results, it is clear that employees who felt a sense of autonomy were motivated to work harder and better, and they were happier while they did it.

This study and many others provide clear direction for people wishing to increase their motivation. It is important to have some control over one's tasks and outcomes. If this situation does not currently exist, then a person should seek other paths that provide more autonomy. Without it, motivation will plummet—and success will become less likely.

Visualize Success

A person might be in a perfect position to pursue a goal. But if that person does not believe that he or she can succeed, there will be very little motivation to act.

This is where a technique called visualization can help. Visualization is not a process of random daydreaming but rather one

Studies have shown that a technique called visualization can help athletes and others achieve their goals. Envisioning success tricks the mind into thinking that the person has actually experienced success, which leads to increased motivation.

of directed, deliberate imagination, in which a person concentrates on mentally experiencing future outcomes in every detail. Athletes, for instance, might envision raising a trophy overhead and hearing the excited crowd chanting their name. They might imagine the sweat cooling on their face and their exhausted muscles trembling a bit, along with the hot flush of victory. Studies have shown over and over that these types of visions actually trick the subconscious mind, which treats them as being true. The athlete has thus "experienced" success, so it becomes believable to him or her—which then increases the athlete's motivation.

Visualization techniques do come with a few scientific warnings. Many studies have shown that imagining success can actually decrease motivation if people focus only on their ultimate goals. Psychologists believe that these fantasies give people a false feeling of achievement that saps their energy to do the hard work of reaching their goals in real life. To be truly motivational, say scientists, visualization must focus not only on the final outcome but also on all the steps needed to get there. "Fantasies that are less positive—that question whether an ideal future can be achieved, and that depict obstacles, problems, and setbacks—should be more beneficial for mustering the energy needed to attain actual success,"[26] explained one scientist in a 2011 study.

Have a Support System

Studies like these point out an uncomfortable fact of life: Big goals usually require big work. Even if the path to success is clear, it probably will not be easy. People who enthusiastically start working toward a goal might find their motivation waning when they encounter obstacle after obstacle.

To keep this from happening, many experts suggest having a support system in place. A support system may consist of friends,

In the Zone

Does a state of perfect motivation exist? Psychologists say it does, and just about everyone has experienced it, at least briefly. Named "flow" by scientist Mihaly Csikszentmihalyi, this state might be described as being "in the zone." It is that moment when a person is completely absorbed in an activity, with a feeling of intent focus, involvement, and enjoyment.

Everyday examples of flow might include the following:

- A tennis player in the middle of an intense volley

- A computer programmer who is so engrossed in writing a piece of code that he or she forgets to eat lunch

- A reader who looks up from a good book and discovers with surprise that two hours have passed

- A video gamer who is trying to defeat a hostile electronic alien

In all of these activities, the individuals have no hesitation or thoughts about whether they should or will do a certain thing. There is only action and perfect engagement in the moment, along with a reduced awareness of the outside world. In this perfect but hard-to-achieve and often short-lived mental space, people are motivated to perform at their peak level—and this in turn allows them to achieve the best possible results.

family, colleagues, or anyone else who will understand and encourage a person's progress. These supporters applaud when things go right and offer reassurance when things go wrong. This type of feedback can boost someone's motivation in difficult moments. As one scientist puts it, "Close supporters not only make us feel cared for and appreciated as we move toward our goals, they also provide a font of motivation. When a new project gets overwhelming and we're ready to scrap it, we think of those who have been our cheerleaders and enablers, and resolve to not let them down."[27]

Having friends with shared goals can be even more motivational. These people are not only cheerleaders, they are also team members. If one member of the team fails, everyone fails—and this fact creates a sense of responsibility that can keep people going when times get tough. An example might be a group of friends who train together to run a team triathlon. One friend trains for the swimming leg, one for the bicycling portion, and one for the run. No one can quit without affecting the other two, and this shared responsibility helps keep the whole group on track. "A natural desire to remain a part of the group and a sense of obligation to its other members is often much stronger than personal reserves of willpower,"[28] explains one researcher.

Stay the Course

Sheer consistency can also shore up a person's willpower and motivation. The basic idea behind this effect is that people do not want to ruin a string of successes. The longer the string, the more motivated they will be to keep it going. A person who quits smoking or drinking alcohol, for example, may feel more and more motivated to abstain as the days, weeks, months, and years roll by. The idea of smoking or drinking again, or "falling off the wagon," after so much success becomes inconceivable.

Comedian Jerry Seinfeld once gave a fan a prime example of this principle. When asked to offer advice to a young comic, he said that the way to succeed was to create better jokes, and the way to create better jokes was to write every single day. To meet this goal, Seinfeld kept a full-year calendar posted prominently on his wall. Each day, after he did his writing, he put a big red X on that square. "After a few days you'll have a chain. Just keep at it and the chain will grow longer every day. You'll like seeing that chain, especially when you get a few weeks under your belt. Your only job next is to not break the chain,"[29] he explained to the fan.

Seinfeld was speaking from personal experience and probably did not have any psychological knowledge to back up his methods. But there is, indeed, ample scientific evidence that staying the course builds motivation. The opposite is also true: Not staying the course has been proved to sap motivation. This principle is known in psychological literature as the abstinence violation effect, and it can be seen in many aspects of everyday life. Anyone who has accepted just one cookie, for example, and abandoned a diet in so doing knows exactly how destructive "breaking the chain" can be to one's motivation.

Regular Rewards

There is another reason that building a chain of successes is so motivational. Each link in the chain—each single day of abstinence, each X on the calendar—is not just part of the larger chain; it also represents one small success. These small successes feel good, and they provide a motivational boost that is strong enough to push a person to the next small goal. One psychologist points out that this effect is what makes online games so addictive. "As you reach each level in Angry Birds or Candy Crush, or get a small win in your game battle or add a piece to your farm, you are motivated to achieve more,"[30] he explains.

It might seem that small motivational boosts like these would not help a person tackle big tasks. But even the biggest accomplishments are made up of many, many smaller steps. By celebrating each small success, people can therefore keep themselves excited about their longer-term goals. "My smaller goals keep me motivated," begins a daily mantra used by one motivational speaker. "Each time I achieve one, I feel rewarded. I am able to see a measurable movement toward the larger, more challenging goals."[31]

An example from everyday life might be an individual who decides to take up weight training as a hobby. At first the person can do only a few repetitions with light weights. Each day, however, he or she manages to do one or two more repetitions. Each week,

> **WORDS IN CONTEXT**
>
> ---
>
> **abstinence violation effect**
> A loss of motivation that occurs as the result of breaking one's commitment to abstain from something.

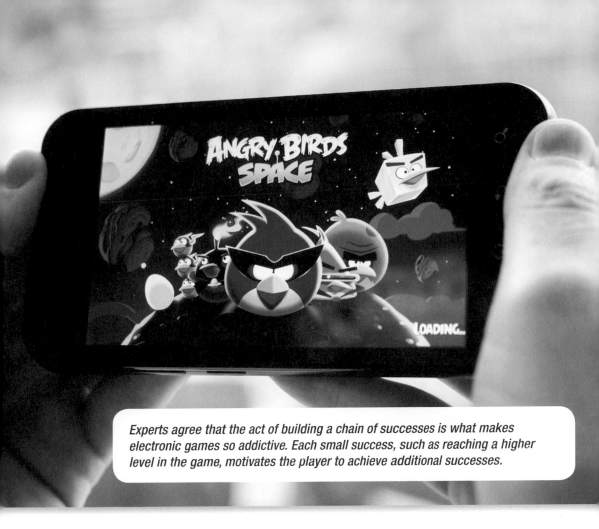

Experts agree that the act of building a chain of successes is what makes electronic games so addictive. Each small success, such as reaching a higher level in the game, motivates the player to achieve additional successes.

the person adds a little more weight. These small successes reward the person and provide the motivation to pursue ultimate fitness goals.

Being the Best

Although small successes and regular rewards are undeniably important, they are useless if they do not support a larger goal. After all, it is not very motivational to lift an extra few pounds of weight if someone has no interest in weight training. It is not very exciting to win a round in a video game if someone thinks online gaming is silly and boring.

When a person has a genuine interest in an activity or outcome, however, the picture changes entirely. Science has shown over and over that people are strongly motivated by the desire to be their best. This idea combines two related concepts: mastery (being very good at something) and self-actualization (reaching one's full potential). The pursuit of these things is intrinsically motivating to most people and can push them to try their hardest.

The key to long-term motivation is therefore not about the daily grind. On one hand, it is important to pick good targets, set goals, have a support system, and do all the other things researchers have found effective. For true long-term motivation, however, science suggests that the best solution is for people to arrange their lives around things that interest them and that they consider valuable. By striving to be their best at all times, in all things, people give themselves the best possible chance of getting and staying motivated.

CHAPTER 5

Profiles in Motivation

There are billions upon billions of people living on earth. Most of them live fairly anonymous lives, unnoticed beyond their own small spheres of connection, and there is nothing unusual about this. On the contrary, it is the norm. It is rare for people to rise above their surroundings in truly extraordinary ways.

For a tiny percentage of humanity, however, this pattern does not hold true. Some people do break free from the pack and distinguish themselves in ways that attract widespread or even worldwide attention. Two things become instantly clear when considering this group: Top performers are all extraordinarily motivated, and this motivation springs from many different sources. Looking at some of the world's most successful people provides an interesting window into the roots of human motivation.

Going for the Gold

It takes incredible work and dedication over long periods of time to become a top athlete. Many people try to excel in their chosen sport, and many fall short. But occasionally an athlete comes along who not only succeeds in being the best but does it in such a dominant way that the whole world takes notice.

This was the case at the 2016 Summer Olympics, when a nineteen-year-old swimmer named Katie Ledecky—the youngest of all 532 athletes on the US Olympic team—blew her competition out of the water. She took home gold medals in all of her individual events, setting two world records along the way and nearly setting a third. And as astonishing as this performance was, observers believe that Ledecky's reign as queen of the swimming

world is only beginning. There is much more to come from this extraordinary athlete.

Ledecky began her competitive swimming career at age six, when her mother signed her up for a local swim team. From the beginning, Ledecky wanted to excel, and she began motivating herself by writing what she called "want times"—speed goals she wanted to achieve for various swimming events—on pieces of paper. That technique has stuck with her to the present day. "I try to set goals that seem kind of unreasonable at first," she explained in a recent interview. "As I work toward them, the more reasonable they look."[32]

Of course, no athlete can reach the top of his or her field without key physical attributes—the right type of body, excellent health, and so forth. Ledecky, like other top athletes, was certainly born with these physical gifts. But according to her coach, Bruce Gemmell, these traits have very little to do with his protégé's ultimate success. "It's not physical, it's between the ears," he says. "It's the absolute, burning desire to get better, and the not being afraid of failure."[33]

Ledecky agrees and says that she did not know at first where this desire to improve would take her. She simply took the first steps, and the rest followed naturally. "I never dreamed I would go to the Olympics when I was 6, 7, or 8 years old. I just started setting goals. And all of a sudden, when I was 14 years old, my next goal was to make the . . . Olympics," she laughs. "I never imagined it."[34]

> ### WORDS IN CONTEXT
>
> #### protégé
> A person who is guided and supported by an older person with more influence and/or experience.

Given her history, however, one can assume that these days Ledecky is imagining what comes next—and it probably includes more gold-medal and world-record finishes. Between her record of successful self-motivation and her willingness to work hard for the things she wants, she has every reason to expect success.

Achieving the Impossible

Success has also become a way of life for Richard Branson, an English entrepreneur who is one of the world's best-known businesspeople due both to his accomplishments and his colorful personality. Born in 1950, Branson started his first business—a magazine—at age sixteen. At age twenty-two, he followed up this venture by founding Virgin Records, an enterprise that eventually grew into a worldwide chain and successful record label.

This feat would have been enough for most entrepreneurs. For Branson, though, it was only the beginning. Endlessly interested in just about everything, Branson used his music business as a springboard into a dizzying array of new areas. In quick succession he started an international airline; took over Britain's railroad transportation system; started a cellular communication company; and most recently, introduced Virgin Galactic, billed as "the world's first commercial spaceline," with the goal of developing ships and carrying tourists into outer space.

This list, while impressive, merely scratches the surface of Branson's ventures. As of 2016 the mogul controlled more than four hundred businesses in thirty different countries. This sprawling and diverse empire is perhaps the inevitable result of Branson's willingness to try anything if it strikes his fancy—which depends partly on whether it seems impossible. If it does, then Branson is all in, for he freely admits that he is irresistibly motivated by difficult tasks. "My interest in life comes from setting myself huge, apparently unachievable challenges and trying to rise above them,"[35] he explained in a 1998 autobiography.

This motivation does not apply only to business. It bleeds into Branson's personal life as well, where it has pushed him to attempt (and earn) a number of world records in areas from ocean crossings to hot-air balloon global circumnavigation. It has also nudged Branson into the arena of humanitarian work, where he has launched a stream of initiatives designed to make the world a better place. It is not easy work, but for Branson that is the entire point of the exercise. Tough is good, daunting is even better, and impossible is the best reason of all to do something. When faced with a task others say cannot be done, this highly motivated individual rolls up his sleeves, grins, and gets to work—and doing so, he has achieved astonishing things.

Doing What You Love

J.K. "Jo" Rowling, the best-selling author of the Harry Potter series, has also achieved astonishing things in a relatively short

Relative Motive Strength

A psychological concept called relative motive strength describes people's different core motivations. The theory holds that some people are very strongly motivated to achieve things, while others are very strongly motivated to avoid failure. The two urges fall at opposite ends of a spectrum, with most people landing somewhere in the middle—sometimes achievement-oriented, sometimes failure-avoiding, depending in part on the specific circumstances.

Not surprisingly, the most successful people tend to have high relative motive strength. This means they have a strong and consistent urge toward achievement and very little fear of failure. They will try almost anything, and they are willing to pour a great deal of effort into big goals, even in the face of repeated obstacles. It might not even cross their minds that failure is a possibility—and if this thought does occur to them, it does not bother them. They do not see failure as a personal flaw, so it does not intimidate them.

There is no doubt that failure can be difficult, even for the most highly motivated people. The trick seems to be acknowledging that failure will hurt but managing not to dwell on the potential pain. By focusing on a positive outcome rather than a negative one, high achievers get the motivation boost they need to accomplish great things.

time. After publishing her first book, *Harry Potter and the Philosopher's Stone* (renamed *Harry Potter and the Sorcerer's Stone* for the US market), in 1997, Rowling found herself caught up in a tidal wave of enthusiasm for all things Potter. Two decades and multiple books later, Rowling has become one of the world's richest women and oversees an empire that includes Potter-related films, theatrical productions, theme parks, merchandise, and much more.

In interview after interview, Rowling has insisted that she never expected this type of success and never sought it. She also says she has never felt motivated by the challenge of creating yet another best seller or earning another big paycheck. Rather, Rowling's only motivation springs from the fact that she loves writing and cannot imagine stopping. The fame and fortune she has

Harry Potter AND THE SORCERER'S STONE

A poster advertises the first movie based on the Harry Potter series of novels by J.K. Rowling. Although the success of the series has made Rowling a billionaire, she says her motivation was the love of writing rather than the pursuit of riches.

earned are merely side effects. "If someone asked for my recipe for happiness, step one would be finding out what you love doing most in the world and step two would be finding someone to pay you to do it. I consider myself very lucky indeed to be able to support myself by writing,"[36] Rowling said in one interview.

Rowling is, of course, gifted with an unparalleled imagination that created the beloved character of Harry Potter along with his magical world and everything in it. Although the seventh and last Harry Potter novel was published in 2007, the "Potterverse" still lives on inside Rowling's head, and to this day the author fights the urge to pick up her pen and produce more Potter books. "It's all still in there. I could definitely write an eighth, ninth, tenth book," she said in a 2010 interview. "I'm not going to say I won't. I don't think I will. . . . I feel I am done, but you never know."[37]

For now, Rowling is channeling her motivation into other subject areas—but she is still writing, and she does not expect she will ever cease. Her intrinsic love of this activity pushes her too hard for quitting to be an option.

She Lives for the Applause

The refusal to quit is also a driving force for Lady Gaga, another artist who has enjoyed an explosive career. Born Stefani Germanotta in 1986, this singer, songwriter, and actress skyrocketed to success following the release of her first album, *The Fame*, in 2008. Today Lady Gaga is known for a catalog of pop hits that includes "Poker Face," "Bad Romance," "Just Dance," "Applause," and many others, as well as for her controversial fashion choices. Outspoken and outrageous, this cultural phenomenon seems endlessly motivated to push the envelope of her art.

This motivation seems to have two main sources. The first is a powerful creative urge and a pure love of making music. If her music career had not taken off, Lady Gaga says, she would still consider herself a success because she would be doing what she adores most. "It was never not going to work out for me because I was already living my dream when I was playing music,"[38] she said in a 2011 interview.

Beyond the music, though, is an even more powerful motivator: Lady Gaga's passionate fan base, which goes by the collective nickname Little Monsters. Lady Gaga frequently mentions her love for her fans and the intense gratification she receives from their adulation. "The monsters are my medicine," Lady Gaga once admitted. "They

> **WORDS IN CONTEXT**
>
> **adulation**
> Extreme, sometimes excessive flattery or praise.

heal me, physically and emotionally, every night at the show. . . . I worship little monsters. They're my religion."[39]

The Little Monsters do not merely sustain Lady Gaga; they push her to continually challenge herself as well. Lady Gaga shed some light on this fact in a 2010 interview when she described her daily routine. "When I wake up in the morning, I feel just like any other insecure 24-year-old girl," she explained. "But I say, 'You're Lady Gaga, you better [expletive] get up and walk the walk today,' because they need that from me. And they inspire

Musician Lady Gaga performs at the Grammy Awards in Los Angeles in 2016. In addition to her love for music, Lady Gaga is motivated by the adulation of her fans, who are known collectively as Little Monsters.

me to keep going."[40] As long as the Little Monsters keep up their end of the bargain, Lady Gaga should have all the motivational fuel she needs to explore new creative realms.

Laughing All the Way to the Bank

A passionate fan base also helps motivate Kim Kardashian West, a reality TV superstar who, as the saying goes, is famous for being famous. Kim got her start in 2007 when her family convinced the E! television network to air a show about their daily life. *Keeping Up with the Kardashians*, which chronicled the everyday lives of Kim, her sisters, and her parents, immediately captivated viewers and became a surprise smash for the network. As of late 2016, twelve seasons of the show had aired, and a thirteenth season was in the works.

From the beginning, Kim emerged as the star of the Kardashian clan. Viewers were drawn to her exotic good looks and genuinely likeable personality. She was more than happy to feed the flames of this interest through a constant social media barrage that included insider tweets, fashion and beauty tips, and selfies—lots and lots of selfies. A circular effect emerged in which the more attention Kim got, the more she shared about herself; the more she shared, the more attention she got; and so on and so on, in a cycle that eventually earned her nearly 50 million followers on Twitter and an astonishing 90 million on Instagram.

Kim is undoubtedly motivated in some part by all this attention. But industry observers, who once viewed her as a self-absorbed, talentless, and somewhat ridiculous figure, have been reaching a new consensus in recent years. Many now believe that she is a marketing genius who is selling her best product—herself—to make as much money as possible and become as famous as possible while she has the chance. It has become clear that Kim is very good at doing these things—and as she herself is quick to point out, it is not an easy job. "I work really hard—I have seven appointments tomorrow before 10am. I'm constantly on the go. I have a successful clothing line. A fragrance," she pointed out in a 2012 interview. "I mean, acting and singing aren't the only ways to be talented. It's a skill to get people to really like you for you, instead of a character written for you by somebody else."[41]

A peek into Kim's bank account proves just how much this particular skill is worth. The star earned an estimated $53 million in 2015 merely for being herself and being willing to share that self on a minute-by-minute basis with her adoring fan base. No one knows what the future may hold, but one can assume that this magnitude of reward will be ample motivation to produce hundreds—even thousands—of social media selfies in the years to come.

A Higher Purpose

Just being herself has also brought fame and fortune to Oprah Winfrey, a multitalented celebrity who seems to dabble in just about everything. Perhaps best known for her daytime talk show that ran from 1983 to 2011, Winfrey is also an award-winning film actress, an author, a philanthropist, a political activist, and much more. Today she keeps busy running the Oprah Winfrey Network on television and *O*, a top lifestyle magazine. All of these ventures have made Winfrey one of the world's most influential people as well as a billionaire several times over.

These results are not due only to hard work, although there has certainly been plenty of that. They also come partly from the fact that Winfrey is blessed with a charismatic personality that attracts positive attention and an enthusiastic, almost cultlike following. Like Kim Kardashian West, Winfrey has used these natural gifts as a springboard to success. Unlike Kim Kardashian West, though, Winfrey is not primarily motivated by material rewards. For her, it is all about following a higher purpose and using her voice to do good in the world. "I wanted to be a teacher. And to be known for inspiring my students to be more than they

A Matter of Perspective

It is an uncomfortable fact of human history that motivation does not always spring from good places. Some of the world's most notorious people have been motivated by extremely negative things. German chancellor Adolf Hitler, for example, burned with a hatred so strong that it motivated him to exterminate an estimated 11 million people. Serial killer Jeffrey Dahmer was motivated by some toxic cocktail of mental illness, genetics, and upbringing to brutally murder seventeen men between 1978 and 1991. And al Qaeda founder Osama bin Laden was motivated by a desire for revenge against the United States, which he held responsible for the oppression and death of countless Muslims through a combination of negligent and malicious foreign policies.

The words *positive*, *neutral*, and *negative* are subjective, of course, and they vary depending on who is applying them. Hitler and Bin Laden both thought their ideals were lofty, and many of their contemporaries agreed with them. Dahmer, on the other hand, seemed to understand that his actions were wrong—but other serial killers genuinely believe that they are helping their victims by releasing them from a painful existence. When it comes to motivation, it seems that the interpretation is all in the eye of the beholder.

thought they could be. I never imagined it would be on TV," Winfrey writes on her website. "I believe there's a calling for all of us. I know that every human being has value and purpose. The real work of our lives is to become aware. And awakened. To answer the call."[42]

Evidence of how motivational this call is for Winfrey comes from a 1997 interview with *Jet* magazine. At this point in her career, Winfrey had been doing her talk show for fourteen years, and she was exhausted. She was thinking about quitting. But then she accepted an acting role in the movie *Beloved*, which dealt with issues surrounding slavery, and something clicked for the superstar. "I realized that I had no right to quit, coming from a history of people who had no voice, who had no power, and that I had been given this—this blessed opportunity to speak to people, to influence them in ways that can make a difference in their lives," she said. "So I came back . . . committed to use the show to change people's lives wherever I could."[43]

The commitment to using her voice and doing good has fueled Winfrey ever since. Piling success upon success, this media mogul has certainly achieved her goal of helping the world—but she is nowhere near finished. As long as there are still people to help, Winfrey's motivation will continue to burn strong.

Many Motivations

Katie Ledecky, Richard Branson, J.K. Rowling, Lady Gaga, Kim Kardashian West, Oprah Winfrey—all are motivated by very different things. For each person, however, the result—a high level of achievement and success—has been the same.

This fact demonstrates that when it comes to getting things done, there is no single correct path. Any type of motivation that propels effort and action will reap results. It is therefore up to each individual to identify his or her unique motivating forces and then build a life around those things. By doing so, every person can set the stage for a successful and satisfying life.

SOURCE NOTES

Introduction: What Is Motivation?

1. Jeffrey S. Nevid, *Essentials of Psychology: Concepts and Applications*. Boston: Cengage Learning, 2014, p. 278.

Chapter 1: Theories of Motivation

2. Daniel H. Pink, *Drive: The Surprising Truth About What Motivates Us*. New York: Riverhead, 2009, p. 18.

3. Pink, *Drive*, p. 18.

4. William McDougall, *An Introduction to Social Psychology*. Boston, MA: Luce, 1909, p. 44.

5. Bre Thurston, "About Bre Thurston Photography," Bre Thurston Photography, 2010. www.brethurston.com.

6. Tina Lifford, "Do You Get Overwhelmed and Leave the Room During Uncomfortable Conversations?," *Huffington Post*, June 26, 2013. www.huffingtonpost.com.

7. Douglas A. Bernstein, *Essentials of Psychology*. Belmont, CA: Wadsworth, 2011, p. 301.

8. Abraham H. Maslow, "A Theory of Human Motivation," *Psychological Review* 50, no. 4, 1943, p. 375.

Chapter 2: Motivation from Without and Within

9. Pink, *Drive*, p. 34.

10. Carol Bainbridge, "Extrinsic Motivation," Verywell, December 16, 2014. www.verywell.com.

11. Quoted in Tom Malinowski, "Call Cruelty What It Is," *Washington Post*, September 18, 2006. www.washingtonpost.com.

12. Quoted in Pink, *Drive*, p. 3.

13. Desirée Rumbaugh, "Seven Ways to Cultivate a Playful, Child-Like Mindset," Desirée Rumbaugh: Love Is Stronger than Fear. www.desireerumbaugh.com.

14. Quoted in Bryan Ramsdale, "Best Halloween Decorations in Wichita," KAKE, October 22, 2016. www.kake.com.

15. Quoted in Kate Borowske, "Curiosity and Motivation-to-Learn," ACRL Twelfth National Conference, 2005. www.ala.com.

16. Quoted in Borowske, "Curiosity and Motivation-to-Learn."

17. Ted Sindzinski, "Why Do People Want to Climb Everest?," Quora, October 27, 2014. www.quora.com.

Chapter 3: The Reward Dilemma

18. Edward L. Deci, "Effects of Externally Mediated Rewards on Intrinsic Motivation," *Journal of Personality and Social Psychology* 18, no. 1, 1971, p. 114.

19. Quoted in Pink, *Drive*, p. 45.

20. F. Warneken & M. Tomasello, "Extrinsic Rewards Undermine Altruistic Tendencies in 20-Month-Olds," *Developmental Psychology* 44, no. 6, 2008.

21. Pink, *Drive*, p. 53.

22. Quoted in Michael Corkery and Stacy Cowley, "Wells Fargo Warned Workers Against Sham Accounts, but 'They Needed a Paycheck,'" *New York Times*, September 16, 2016. www.nytimes.com.

Chapter 4: Getting and Staying Motivated

23. Kendra Cherry, "5 Surprising Ways to Get Motivated," Verywell, September 14, 2015. www.verywell.com.

24. Jim Rohn, "4 Tips for Setting Powerful Goals," *Success*, June 28, 2015. www.success.com.

25. Alex Lickerman, "The Desire for Autonomy," *Psychology Today*, May 6, 2012. www.psychologytoday.com.

26. Heather Barry Kappes and Gabriele Oettingen, "Positive Fantasies About Idealized Futures Sap Energy," *Journal of Experimental Social Psychology* 47, 2011, p. 728.

27. Jeff Wise, "The Tough Track," *Psychology Today*, March 15, 2011. www.psychologytoday.com.

28. Wise, "The Tough Track."

29. Quoted in Gina Trapani, "Jerry Seinfeld's Productivity Secret," *Lifehacker* (blog), July 24, 2007. www.lifehacker.com.

30. Ronald E. Riggio, "5 Ways to Infect Others with Motivation," *Psychology Today*, March 23, 2014. www.psychologytoday .com.

31. Success Praxis, "Mantra for Achieving Your Goals," August 18, 2016. www.successpraxis.com.

Chapter 5: Profiles in Motivation

32. Quoted in Philip Hersch, "Chasing Katie Ledecky," ESPN, August 4, 2016. www.espn.com.

33. Quoted in Hersch, "Chasing Katie Ledecky."

34. Quoted in Margaret Warner, "At the Pool with Freestyle Phenom Katie Ledecky," *PBS NewsHour*, August 25, 2016. www .pbs.org.

35. Richard Branson, *Losing My Virginity: How I Survived, Had Fun, and Made a Fortune Doing Business My Way*. New York: Crown Business, 2011, p. 194.

36. Amazon, "Magic, Mystery, and Mayhem: An Interview with J.K. Rowling," 1999. www.amazon.co.uk.

37. J.K. Rowling, interviewed by Oprah Winfrey, *The Oprah Winfrey Show*, ABC, October 1, 2010.

38. Quoted in Derek Blasberg, "Lady Gaga: The Interview," *Harper's Bazaar*, April 13, 2011. www.harpersbazaar.com.

39. Quoted in Shari Weiss, "Lady Gaga Interviewed by Elton John for *V* Magazine: My Fans Are 'My Medicine, My Religion,'" *New York Daily News*, May 13, 2011. www.nydailynews.com.

40. Quoted in Neil Strauss, "The Broken Heart and Violent Fantasies of Lady Gaga," *Rolling Stone*, July 8, 2010. www.roll ingstone.com.

41. Quoted in Emma Brockes, "Kim Kardashian: My Life as a Brand," *Guardian* (Manchester, UK), September 7, 2012. www.theguardian.com.

42. Oprah Winfrey, "Every Person Has a Purpose," *O, the Oprah Magazine*, November 2009. www.oprah.com.

43. Quoted in *Jet*, "Oprah Winfrey Reveals the Real Reason She Stayed on TV," November 24, 1997, pp. 59–60.

FOR FURTHER RESEARCH

Books

Dan Ariely, *Payoff: The Hidden Logic That Shapes Our Motivations*. New York: Simon & Schuster, 2016.

Jack Canfield and Janet Switzer, *The Success Principles: How to Get from Where You Are to Where You Want to Be.* 10th anniversary ed. New York: William Morrow, 2015.

Sean Covey, *The 7 Habits of Highly Effective Teens: The Ultimate Teenage Success Guide*. New York: Simon & Schuster, 2014.

Brian Grazer, *A Curious Mind: The Secret to a Bigger Life*. New York: Simon & Schuster, 2016.

Jackie Huba, *Monster Loyalty: How Lady Gaga Turns Followers into Fanatics*. New York: Portfolio/Penguin, 2013.

Daniel H. Pink, *Drive: The Surprising Truth About What Motivates Us*. New York: Riverhead, 2009.

Sean Smith, *Kim Kardashian*. New York: HarperCollins, 2015.

Gregory Zuckerman, *Rising Above: How 11 Athletes Overcame Challenges in Their Youth to Become Stars*. New York: Philomel, 2016.

Websites

Mind Tools (www.mindtools.com). This site offers a wealth of practical tools to increase motivation and boost productivity in all areas of life.

Oprah.com (www.oprah.com). The motivational queen offers her insights on ways to live better, find personal joy and success, and improve the world.

Psychology Today (www.psychologytoday.com). This website supports the magazine of the same name. It offers easy-to-understand articles on many psychological topics, including motivation.

Tony Robbins (www.tonyrobbins.com). Motivational guru Tony Robbins offers his unique perspectives and advice on his personal website.

Verywell (www.verywell.com). The psychology section of this health information website contains a wealth of interesting, well-written articles covering many aspects of motivation.

INDEX

PICTURE CREDITS

Cover: Depositphotos.com/Greg Epperson

6: Maury Aaseng

9: Thinkstock Images/Jetta Productions

13: akg-images

18: Depositphotos.com/xprmntl

24: Shutterstock.com/John Kropewnicki

27: Depositphotos.com/monkeybusiness

31: Depositphotos.com/prudek

37: Depositphotos.com/photography33

41: iStock.com/jetcityimage

50: iStock.com/strickke

55: iStock.com/formicamonkey

58: Depositphotos.com/frinz

62: © Warner Bros. Pictures/Photofest

64: PG/Splash News/Newscom

ABOUT THE AUTHOR

Kris Hirschmann has written more than four hundred books for children. She owns and runs a business that provides a variety of writing and editorial services. She lives just outside Orlando, Florida, with her husband, Michael, and her daughters, Nikki and Erika.